New Faces of China

New Faces of China

by Willis Barnstone

Indiana University Press

Bloomington and London

Published in Canada by Fitzhenry & Whiteside Limited, Don Mills, Ontario

Library of Congress catalog card number: 73-81160

ISBN: 0-253-15660-2

Manufactured in the United States of America

Cover photographs by Willis Barnstone, and reprinted by permission
of *Holiday Magazine* ©1973

for Bernard Perry

The light of China, like the landscape,
is vast yet intimate. The poems and paint-
ings of early dynasties show mountains
that suddenly emerge from mist and rain
or stand in the intimate beauty of full
sunlight or moonlight. So the Tang poet
and painter Wang Wei (701-761) wrote:

The river flows beyond the sky and earth.
The mountain's color, between seen and unseen.

To the camera eye—that can deal only
with physical light—China presents end-
less varieties of light experience. To
the human eye, the changing rays over
odd shapes of mountains, the Great Wall,
the calligraphic orchards, cause us
to adjust our lens, to change aperture
and depth of field—as the world looms
and fades. To be in China is to alert
one's eyes to constant visual surprise.
When the camera looks at people, it is
not, in a deeper sense, different from
focusing on the land. The people are
natural, unposed, almost incapable of
posing. Yet an intense concentration—
perhaps reflecting a contemporary mood—
illuminates a face, even the fresh, intense laughter of the children. How can
one be natural yet intense? Fresh yet
anciently wise? Of today yet also of
antiquity? These contradictions are China.
To ignore them is to walk blind in the
Middle Kingdom. To see China, then, is
to operate through the paradoxes of time.

Time—or shutter speed of the camera—
is behind each person, unpolluted mountain
or rice paddy. While no nation in our
century has undergone a more radically
pervasive socio-political change, nowhere
is the measuring eye of historical time
more critical to understanding. Present
accomplishments are visible in the light
of a feudal past. That past is not dead
but transformed. Not family, warlord
and emperor, but family, comrade and
state. Not ancestor worship but aus-
tere faith in an improving future.

Moreover, these ethical obsessions of
the Chinese people persist in familiar
ways. Confucius has given way to Mao's
poems and maxims. The traditional le-
galists decree "correct" political think-
ing. As in the past, however, an unfail-
ing sense of historical movement, of
accommodation, of wisdom and patience,
persist as a necessity for survival.
In a land of swiftly changing light
and politics, the Chinese ethical pos-
ture, constant yet flexible, carries
the nation through time.

This bright ethical alertness in the
spirit of the people shows itself on
the faces—of schoolchildren, workers,
old peasants. In China one is awake.
Foreigners note this, and comment on
the enormous energy of contemporary
life. People look busy. Perhaps this
energy, the "struggle for production,"
the "continuing revolution" account for
the enthusiasm expressed by many recent
visitors, of the left and right, for the
new China.

The new China is seen most clearly and
poignantly in the children. Their good
health is like a newly washed shirt in the
sun. The austerity of adult uniforms
gives way among the children to print blouses,
crazy-quilt dresses, and elaborate hairdos.
Their faces are stained with rouge and lipstick when they perform regional dances in
Tibetan or Islamic costumes. Yet their
hundred moods reveal the complexity of a
child's spirit. Notions of stereotyped
automatism are frequently offered to explain
the extraordinary changes of recent decades.
The reductive concepts vanish on the profound faces of the children as their moods
move from sadness and wonder to playfulness
and absent gazing.

And to be awake in Jong Gwo (the Middle
Kingdom) is not, as in traditional
India, to intuit unmeasurable eternity
beyond the earth. Rather it is to see
historical man and landscapes of our
world. In the poems of Sappho, on her
white island of Mytilene, light fell on
her house, in her time, illuminating her
villages, olive trees and friends.
Aphrodite was a companion not a god.
Greece and China—so far from eternity
and close to history—have been the most
active creators and recorders of the
things of our world. To see China—or
Greece—through the camera eye is a just
privilege. For China lives under a
physical light, looming and fading
outside and—from an ancient and
ethical interior—burning itself
upon the features of its people.

the Chinese grip
is invincible

I am so still
that time forgot to

tick. yet the jade
tablet in my head

is bright with thought
in all 4 tones

girls sing
joyfully

but the
violinist

suffers
for art

my sky
in a

Shanghai
day nursery

is made
of planets

do you know what
I see? you. I

look through your face
and see my ivory

teeth and a glaze
of light. we are

friends. I don't worry.
we are like marble

shining in the earth
from Greece to China

raining from a cliff
of plum blossoms

is the applause for
our art. in

a second we go out
to drink music

the Great Wall
crawls over China

light lies on
the rock serpent

O come and go. You, still half a child,
fill out the dance-figure for a moment
to the pure constellation of one of those
dances in which we fleetingly transcend

dumbly ordering Nature.

Rainer Maria Rilke
Sonnets to Orpheus, B 28

we 3 sit
under gold tiles

of the once
Forbidden City

tall as white ghosts
he looks

at a red pumpkin
and hopes

the harmony of 2
+ 2 + 2

equals all the tall songs
on stars

where he performs with grace
and make-up

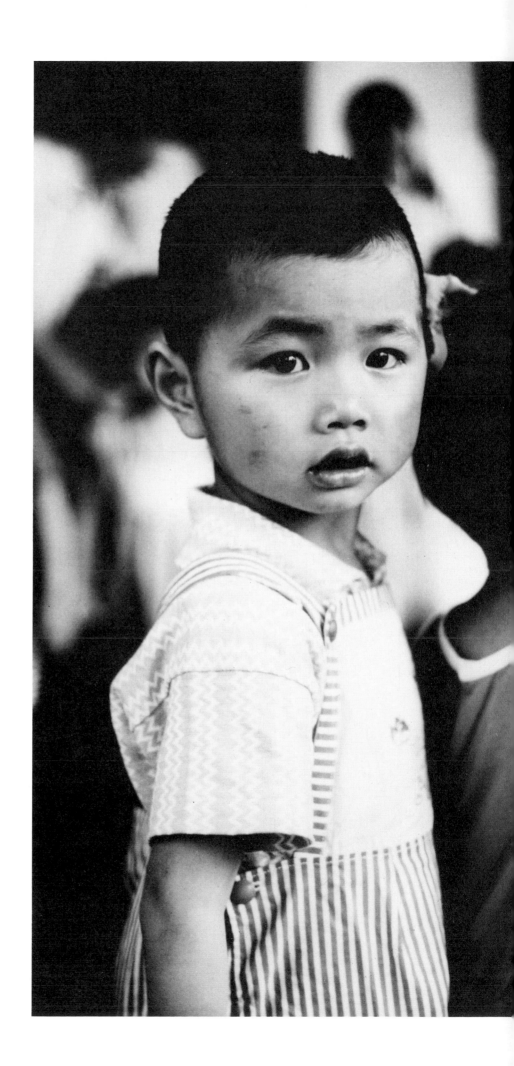

on the eighth day
in the garden

we watered
the world

weeds talked
like parrots

I watched eagerly
my watering can

showered water
on cucumbers

I carry a flower
growing big in Shanghai

I made the flower
of paper and lettuce

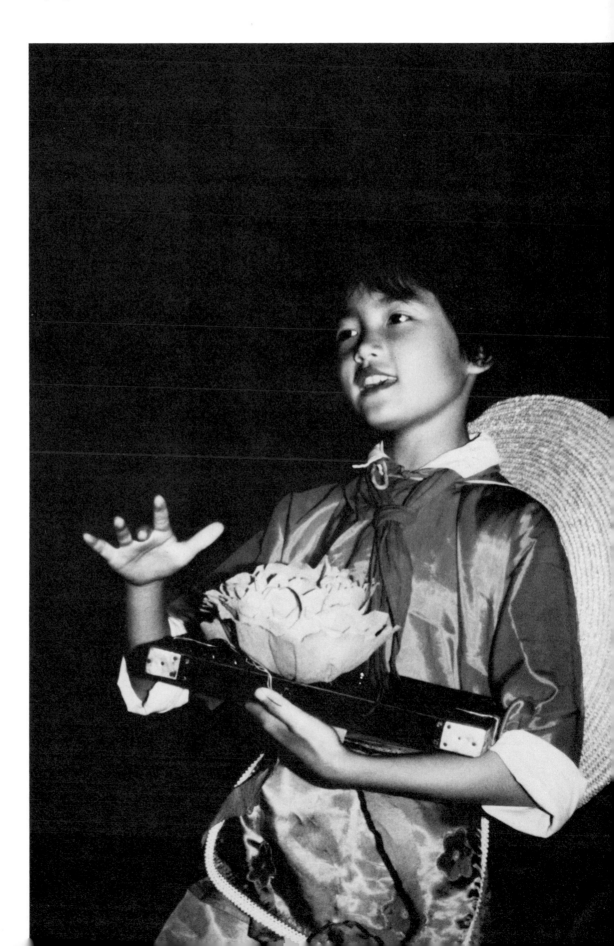

only a mirror
is strong enough

to catch the
moon. 3 unicorns

cannot be trapped.
they pass over

the earth's meadows
like wild daisies

we are amazed
thanks
the last time we saw a man
on the ground
he was shiny
pulled by strings
and dressed like a dragon

you are crazy
but we like you

the dragon's
mouth is

open in the
Forbidden City.

Eden went
to Peking

and no one
got in

but emperors
and friends

puppets dance for
the revolution and
for the liberation

I am faithful
and calm like

clouds over a
Taoist hill top

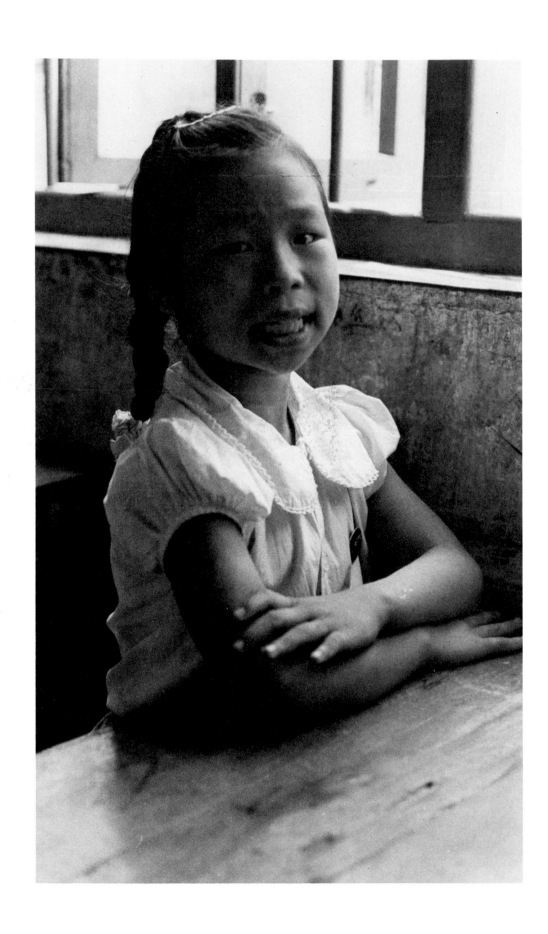

her teeth
are not lace or swans

her eyes
are mother-of-pearl

in which
quarter moons got lost

a bobby pin
a plow in the light

the moons
stare and you are seen

red lips
and ribbons

of Red
Guard girls

gaze. eyes
and teeth

buttons, badges,
hair, white

shirts dance
and laugh

We have a little sister
and she has no breasts.
What will we do for our sister
when they ask for her hand?
If she is a wall
we will build a turret of silver on her.
If she is a door
we will enclose her with boards of cedar.

The Song of Songs

to us you
are funny

on the floor
of our

day nursery
in Changsha

smiling
is easy

through the window
I see the

myna bird talk
in his cage.

my mother drank
orange soda. then

she floated like
candy smell and

came by to
tie my hair

In the factories at eight in the morning
the workers study poems of the Old Man

but in the courtyard you put on lipstick
and rouge and dance minority dances,

and we play pingpong. You win. Then I jump
on the highbar and everyone crawls out

of the walls to see! You bounce more than I
do. After coins drop out of my pocket

I spin, do a few kips, and finally hang
perilously from my heels. Then it's tea time

and I and you, four kids in the third grade,
write poems. The teachers cheat a bit, slipping

you words and strokes. But we are all clearly
great artists. And besides, we made a pact;

I'll swing on the highbar any day for
tea and poems. You'll write them any good day

for friendship. You clap when I leave. I hope
you always remember our pact. I will.

my work by a tea-
commune-big-puddle

is to sit alone
and play with water.

the world is puddle
wonderful, a poet

sang. my games and thought
are better than words.

I and my shadow
are alone in China

3 eyes
2 have black ships
1 a black wave

of a deep sea

because I am a panda
I don't call

the woodcutter for company
as he walks

by my cold mountain in Tibet.
I let black snow

shine in my eyes. my duty
is to play

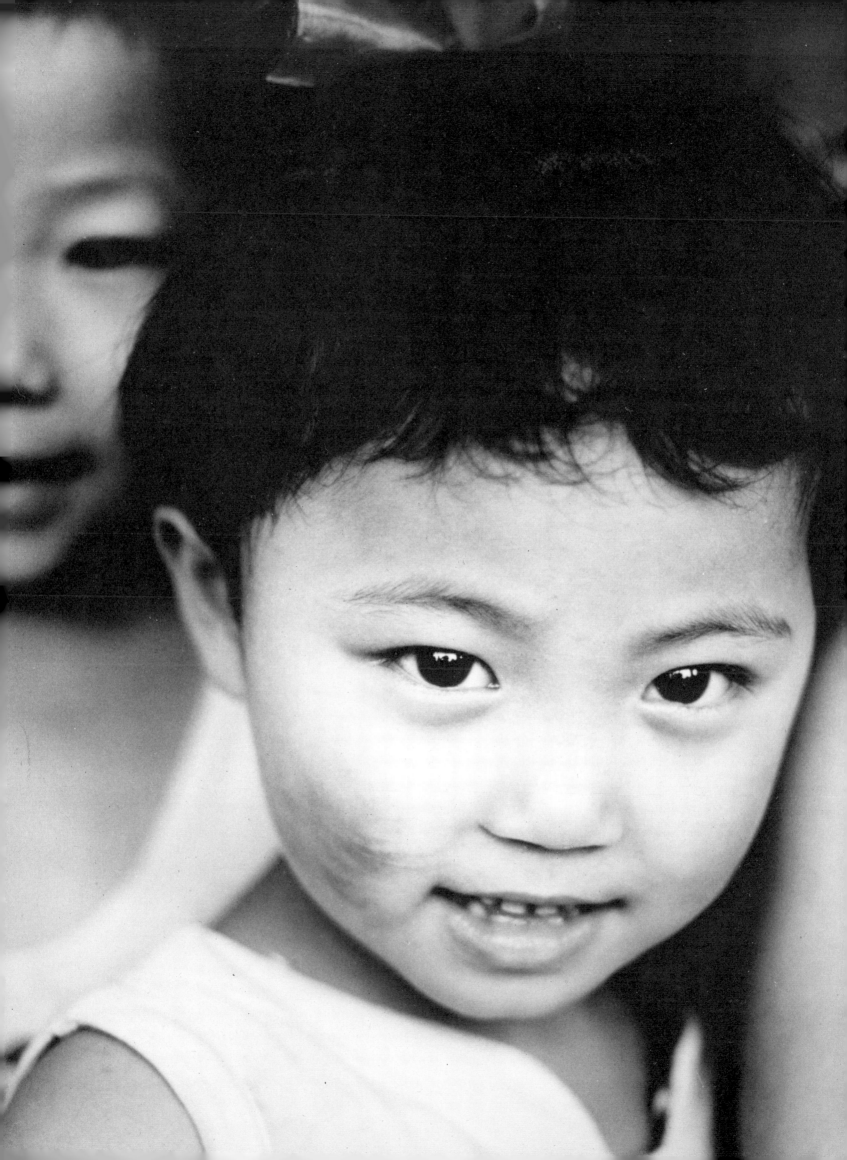

he is serious
with hands down

her ribbon
flew out

of Inner
Mongolia like

geese against
the full

moon. the
ribbon asked

the sun
under her

eyes for
one star

from her
pupil. she

said yes

The Red Army is not afraid of hardship on the march,
   the Long March.
Ten thousand waters and a thousand mountains are
   nothing.
The Five Sierras meander like small waves,
the summits of Wumeng pour on the plain like balls
   of clay.
Cliffs under clouds are warm and washed below by the
   River Gold Sand.
Iron chains are cold, reaching over the Tatu River.
The far snows of Minshan only make us happy
and when the army pushes through, we all laugh.

October 1935
Mao Tse-tung

Shaoshan. Mao was
born here and

learned how to
swim and take

sun and rain
baths on the

mountains. it helped
 (he told Edgar

Snow) get strong
for the Long March

Mao Tse-tung
lives in Hangjo

where old poets
often wrote about

the beauty of
the West Lake

the masses pose for
photos by West Lake

where they go for
tea or cold beer.

elegant trees and Chinese
roofs. trousers. slow time

Canton. I am
serene. one eye
laughs. guess?

old men out at dawn
shadow box *(tai chi)*

with an invisible sword
or jog in shorts,

in the streets or
in the Middle School

China does push-ups
and stays healthy. a

basketball clinic is popular
and better for girls

than brocade or broken
ankles. the acrobats fly

over horses and myths
like perfect calligraphy

I wear fancy
clothes, lace

polka dots,
and raise

my thoughts
on high

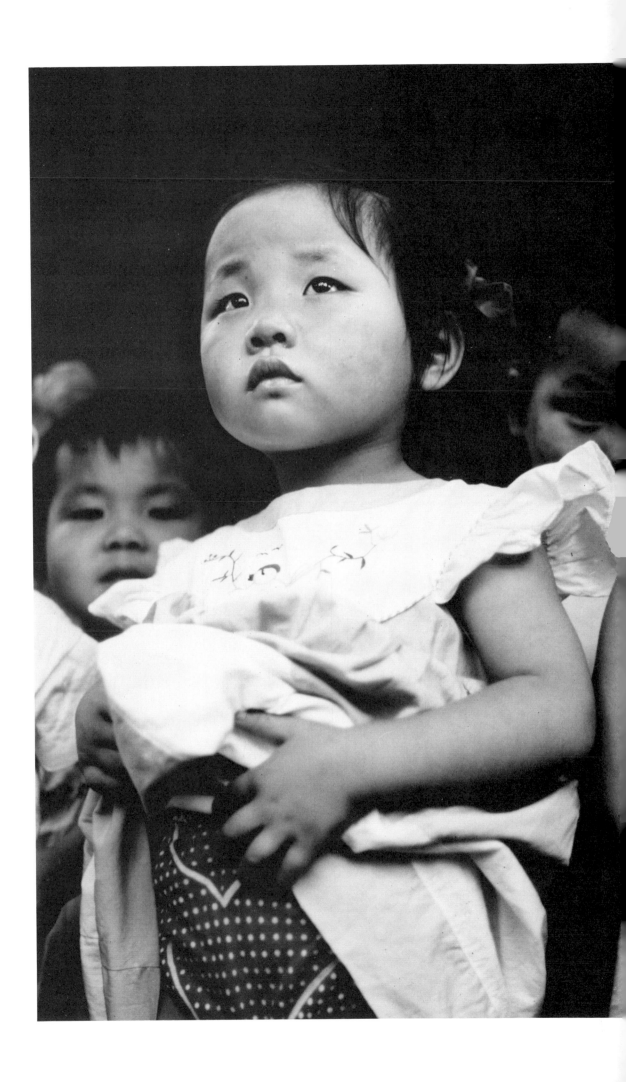

my cheeks shiny like
balloons of milk

in my head are
2 black cypresses

in Hunan people
like hibiscus in

the morning, peppers
at noon. now

rowing through
the river light

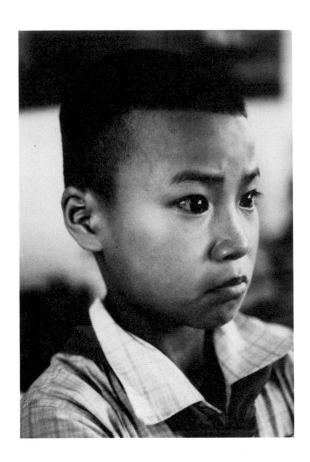

I am a
responsible

citizen
with black

jade in
my eyes

and sweat on
my nose

healthy as
the sun.

my hair
is wind

only the Arabs sometimes
lend numbers

for algebra. all the rest
goes back to

oracle bones and tortoise
shells where

the first pictograms were
scratched. Greeks

used the tortoise shell
for the lyre

and harmony. the Chinese
drew pictures

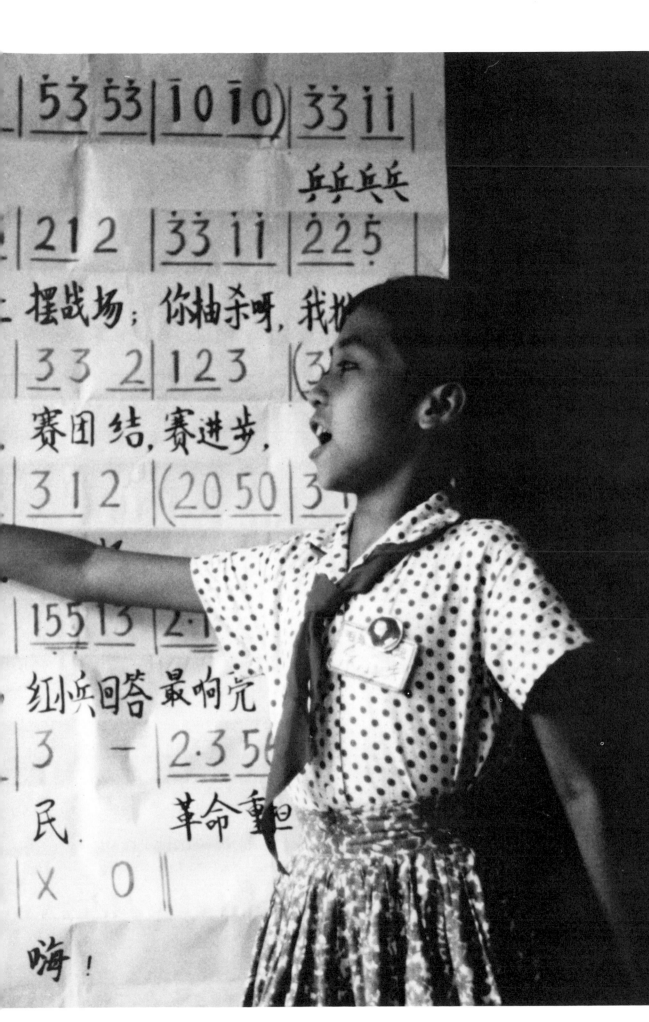

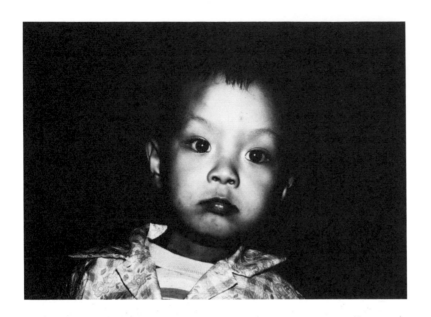

worker's apartment in
Shanghai. boy with

2 full moons
in his eyes

first came
the ancient Yellow Emperor

I see 10,000 miles

Genghis Khan knew only how to bend
his bow
and hunt the eagle

he vanished like snow

I worry about hard paths
up a mountain of black jade

I am myself
easily profound

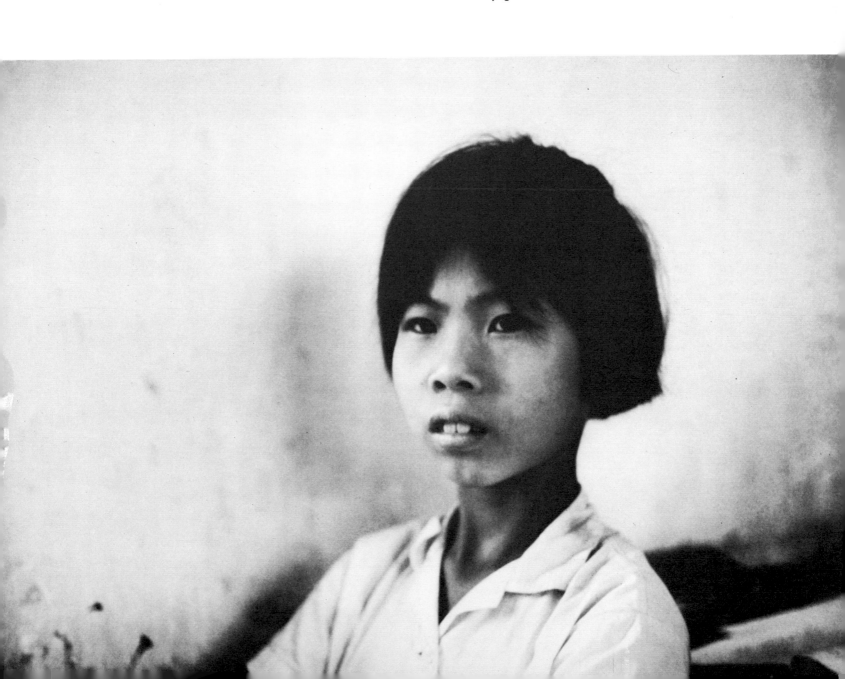

I work hard
with my blocks

to build socialism
yet all is

not easy for
a thoughtful man

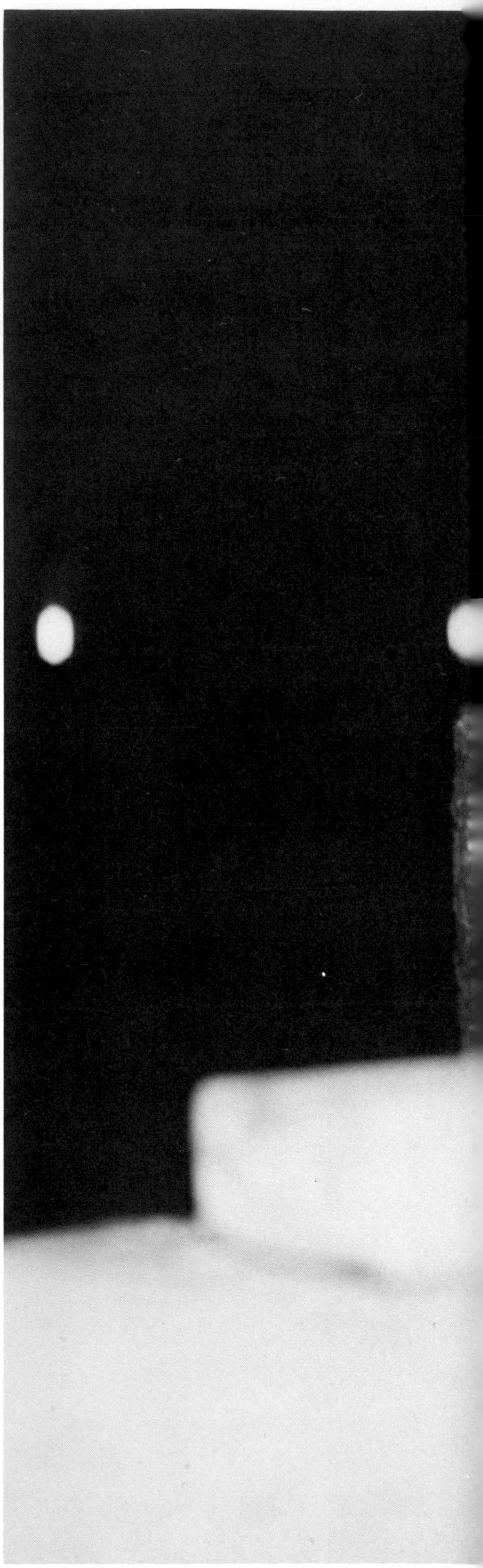

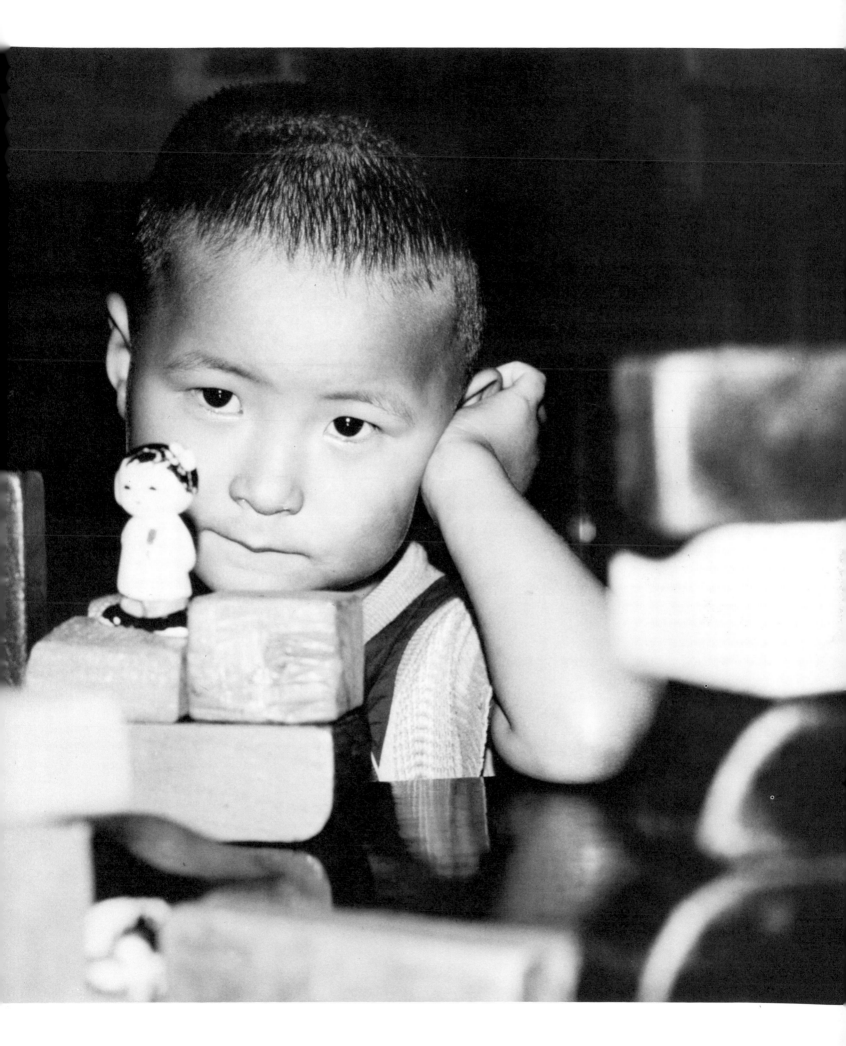

when I get
big I'll be

an engineer, boxer
or bottom man

holding acrobats. my
friend has a silly

laugh but my
thoughts are maps—

hills on my forehead,
seas in my eyes

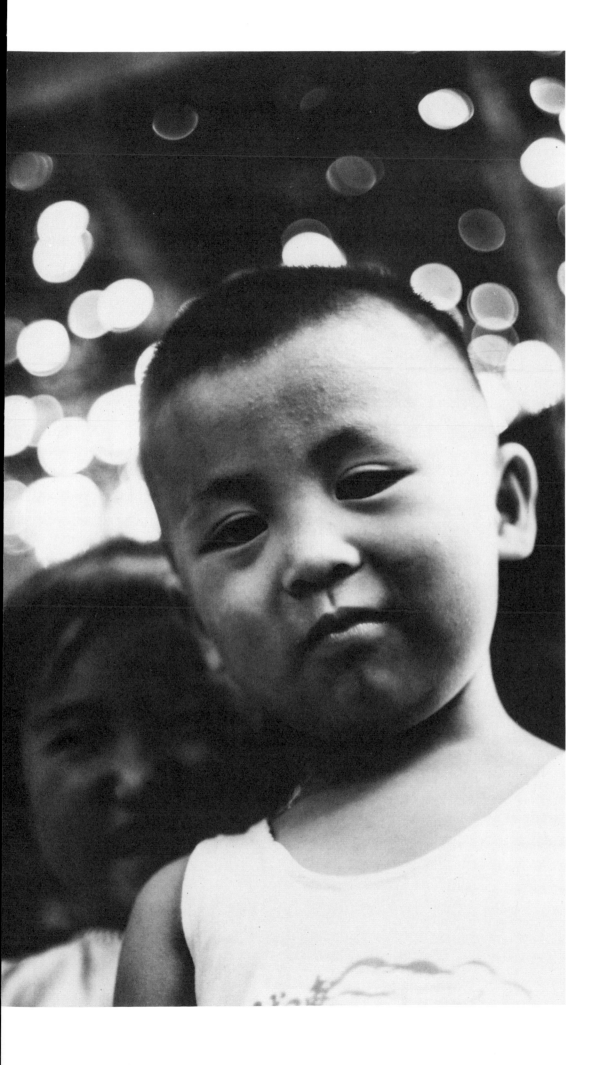

in Hunan province
in central China

he fishes alone
in his black

shirt. he holds
a white tree

in the Hsiang
River a man

struggles to free
his junk stuck

in sand off
Orange Island where

Mao as a boy
swam with friends

I wonder. I dream
please. say nothing

I wonder. I dream

in Peking 2 bikes,
1 pedibike truck

and a few Russians
on the walls, Lenin

& Stalin, and cars
far off. Peking

is glory. wind of
red dust and acacias

I emerge from darkness
and shine. if you ask in dead night
who I am, look
carefully.
clearly
clouds are not in my heart

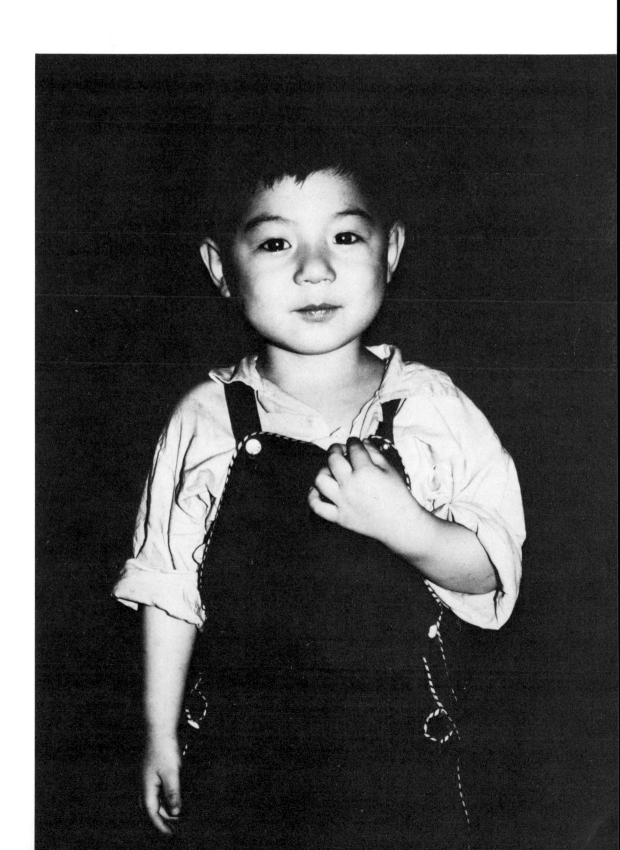

Altar of Heaven
in Peking where

the Emperor, the
Son of Heaven,

came at winter
solstice to prostrate

himself for the
redemption of mankind

a hot thermos
and tea leaves

are everywhere: in
trains, hotel rooms.

a guest drowns
in green tea.

here in Hangjo
on a commune

peasants pick
the glaucous leaves

ice cream at
Peking zoo

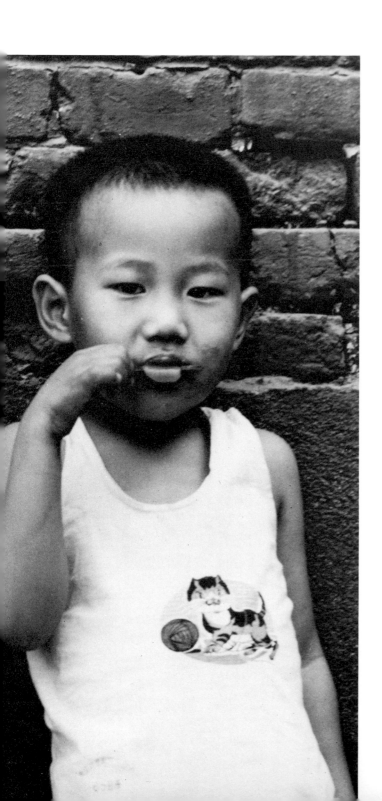

But as I rav'd and grew more fierce and wilde
   At every word,
Me thought I heard one calling, *Child!*
   And I reply'd, *My Lord.*

George Herbert (1593-1633)
"The Collar"

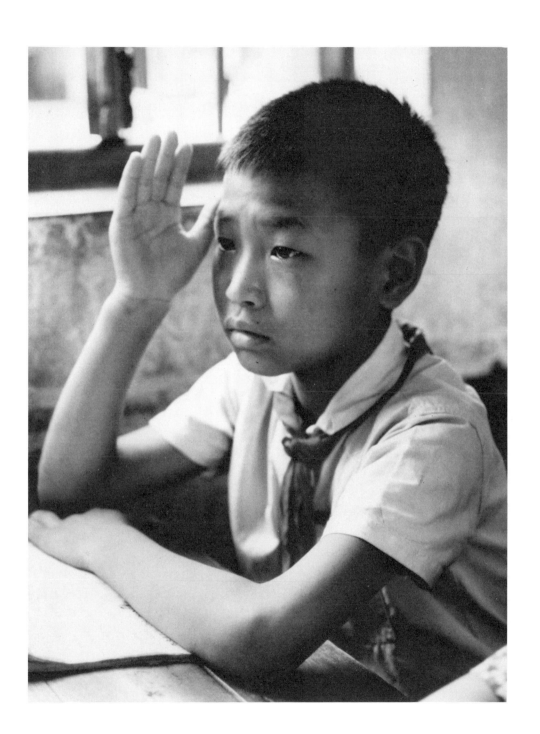

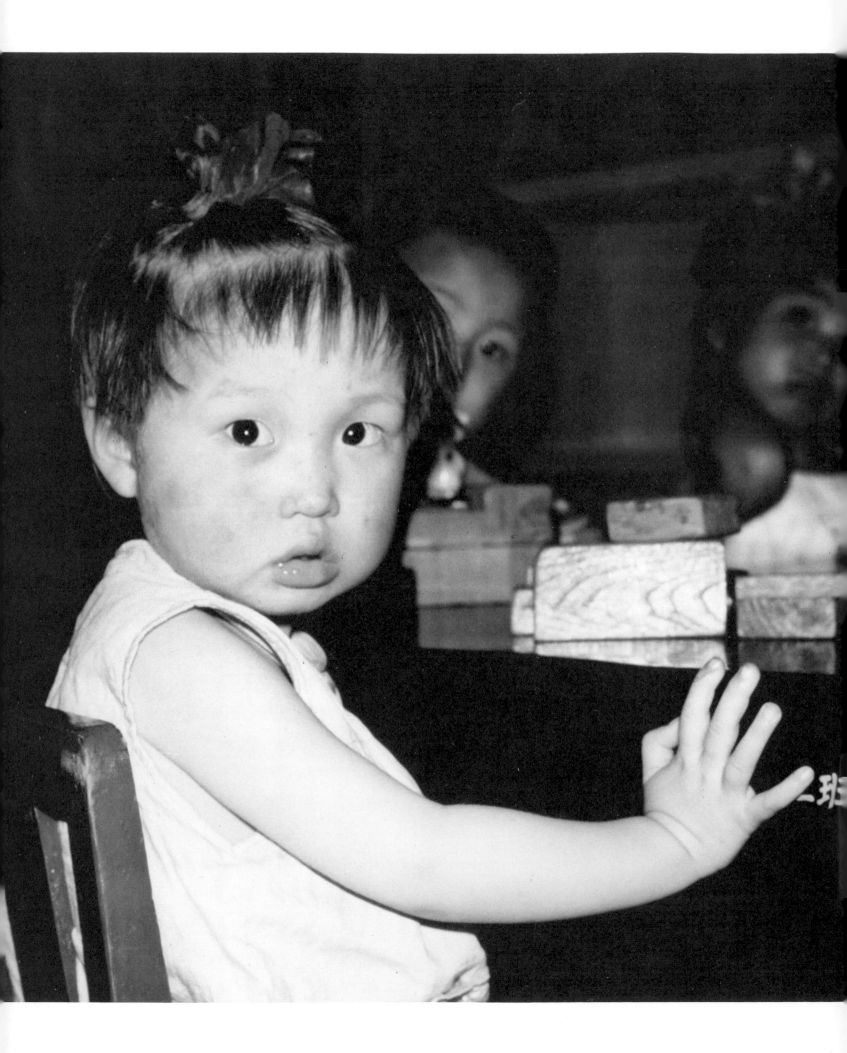

I do not have a rancourous spirit
but the simple heart of a child.

Sappho

I put on rouge
before I dance

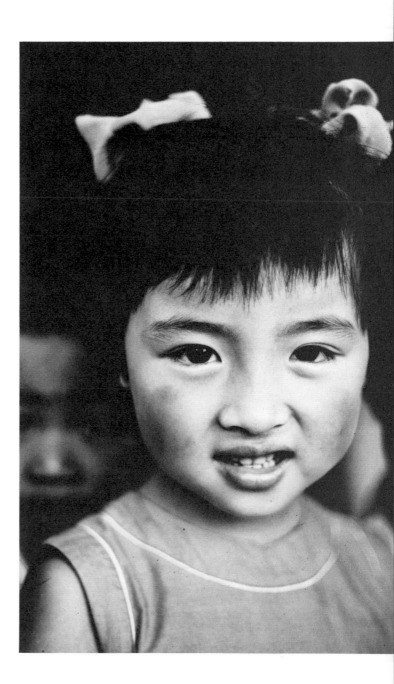

in the biggest square
on the planet

her white sock is a column
to vaguery

she owns the square
her friend a bike

a cock tugs
at the morning breeze

they sit casually
in a shadow

a Mandarin stands
on the earth,

the road to
where 13 emperors

lie buried in
the Ming Tombs

we smile
sideways

dancing
minority

dances in
Canton

my shirt says
what my eyes

say: smooth sailing
over rough seas

out of dust
I was made

I look at
a new earth

where silk worms
fly like geese

and dust is
water for rice

she is amused
I wonder

where are you from?
she knows

my thought drops
deeper than maps

of the sea
where blue fish

swim to a castle.
my thought climbs

like polo shirts
in intense light

I see you
with 1 eye

and 100 fingers.
eyes are deep

by the wall
by the light

I am alone
with a wonder

Lao Tzu said
there's a way

he is little
but his fingers clean
the air

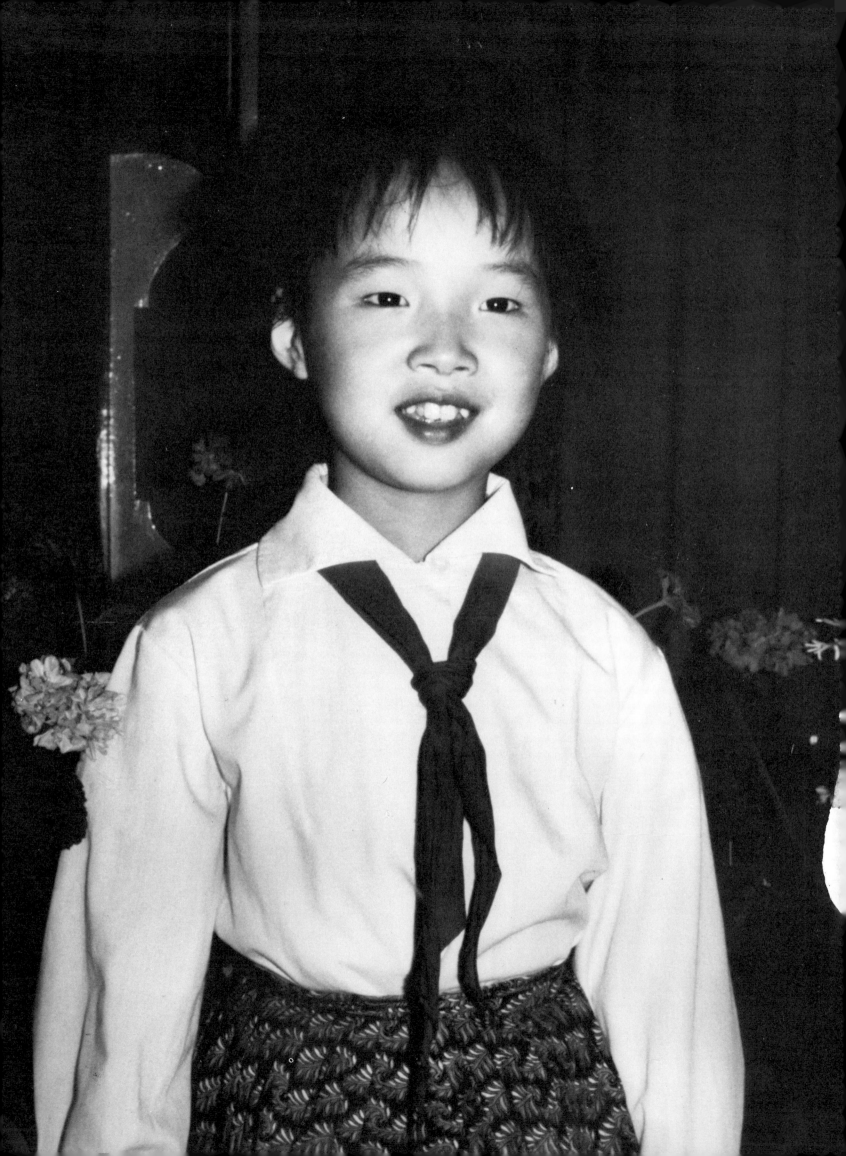

nothing can surprise
my hands. even when

the sea has no light
under shining porpoises

in a school of
many friends

I found the time
to let my arms

in the dark corner
talk. they say, one

of the friends is
you. I stand

knowing I am one
and many. hello

in Chinese schools
English is studied

replacing Russian. here
is lesson twenty-nine

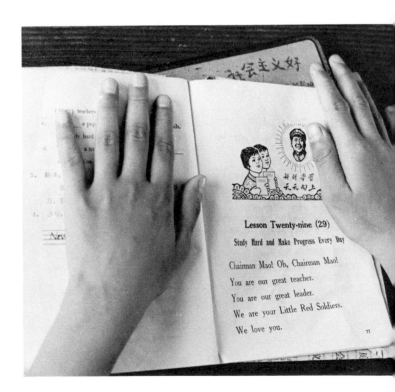

sun on
his lower lip

proves
the tear

in each eye
is a tiny

solitude
of sun

yes I am delicate
and alert like my shirt

my ribbon is a bell
of light in a gorge

yes I am delicate
and alert

in Hangjo even
arms and trees

are calligraphic
strokes of nature

my pajamas are not
sad. nor is the

girl behind me. she
is a blurred deer.

but I am sad
and thoughtfully clap

my face
thought.

one half
smiles

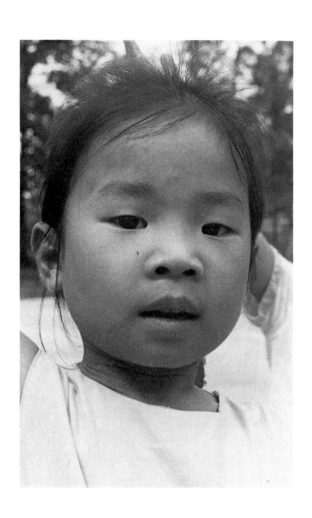

above this mountain village
a Buddhist shrine

in my hand the straw sun
of the Incas

in my bag a poem of folly
and my lunch

natural
to dance. the

earth is better
when it spins.

in a Chinese
jump-dance

we quiver
like red flowers

toward morning
light. we

breathe better
when the earth

spins. it is
natural

for sun & moon
to dance

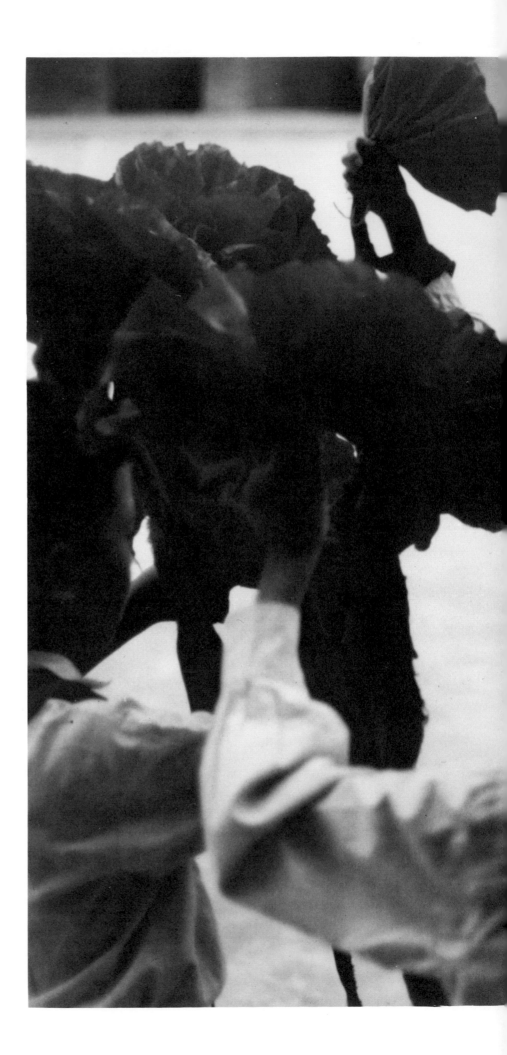

in sneakers and bluejeans
I play a round cucumber

that fell from a ship
of mulberry leaves. if

you look at my fingers
skillfully, please see

that each is tense, graceful
and sculpted like music

welcome. a sweet
smile from my

friend. his shirt
is clean cotton

that blows about
like ancient silk.

in the morning
the rain bird,

shang yang, came
to wash his eyes

a boy in the gardens
of the imperial city

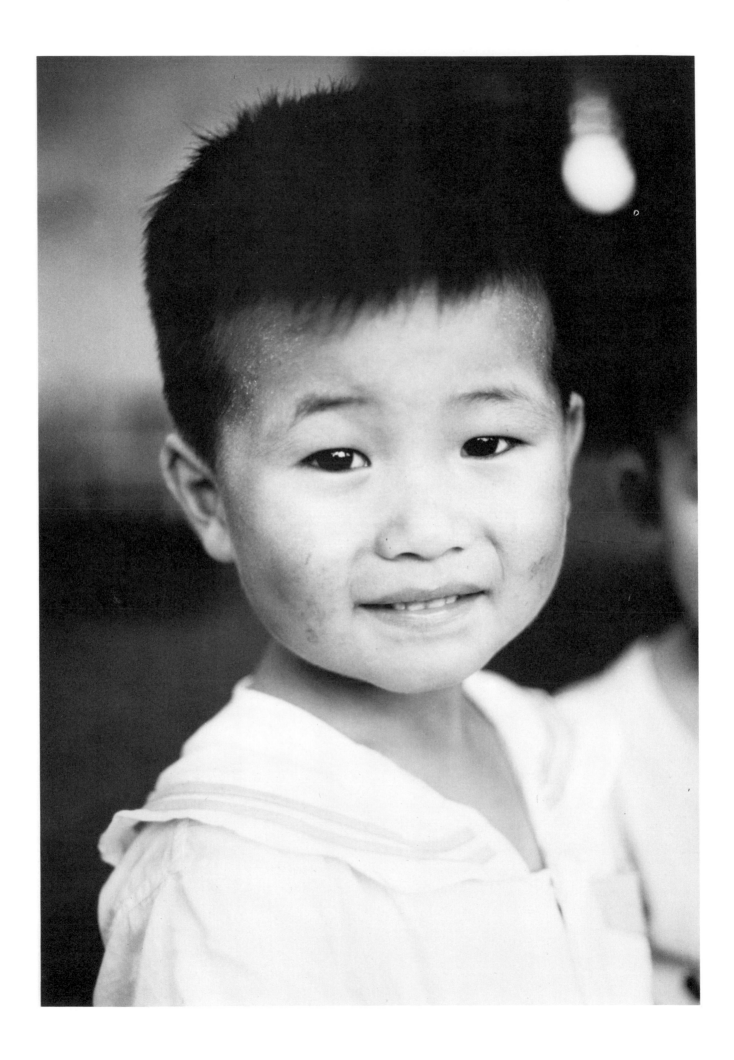

a boy in a
sailor suit is

temporarily
on shore. an orange

tree on the hill
is his sun. he

charts the evening sea
in his room

by one electric
bulb overhead.

outdoors at night
a ship of clouds

in my clean dress
I learn to be

a peasant. my fingers
are five hills of rain

we are
happy

the word innocent
means nothing. you

came and now
we understand. welcome

we read Chinese
it isn't easy

the teacher asks
who are the

model emperors? who
are Shun & Yao?

what does scarlet
rain mean in

Chairman Mao's poem
about peach blossoms?

my hair knows the secrets
of galaxies

my friend the water buffalo
cools it

under water where the mud
is icy soft

generations of birds hover
like bright cheese

in light between sierras
under my hair

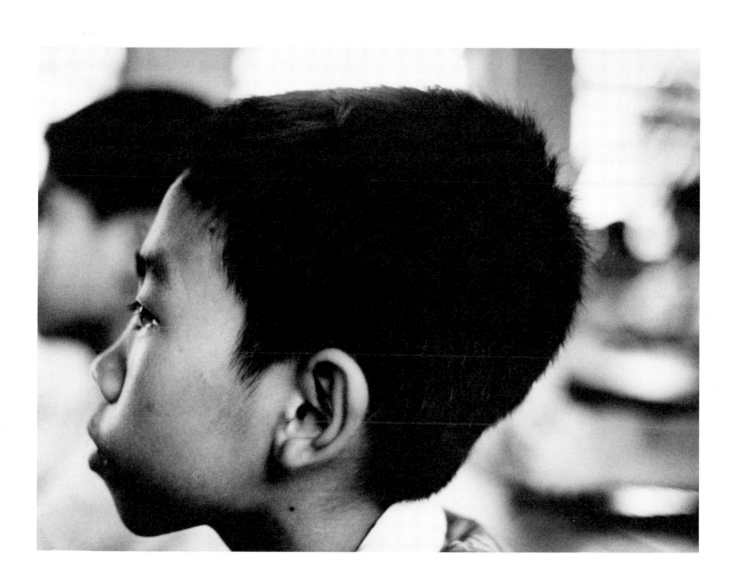

how carefully
his arms cradle the air
with correct gestures
his eyes
look out almost
and look down up inward
and his meditation
is held back by his mouth
how correct and severely
gentle

for 10,000 years
we walk in

the rice paddies
where seedlings feed

the masses with
an eternal snow

of white proteins
that never melts

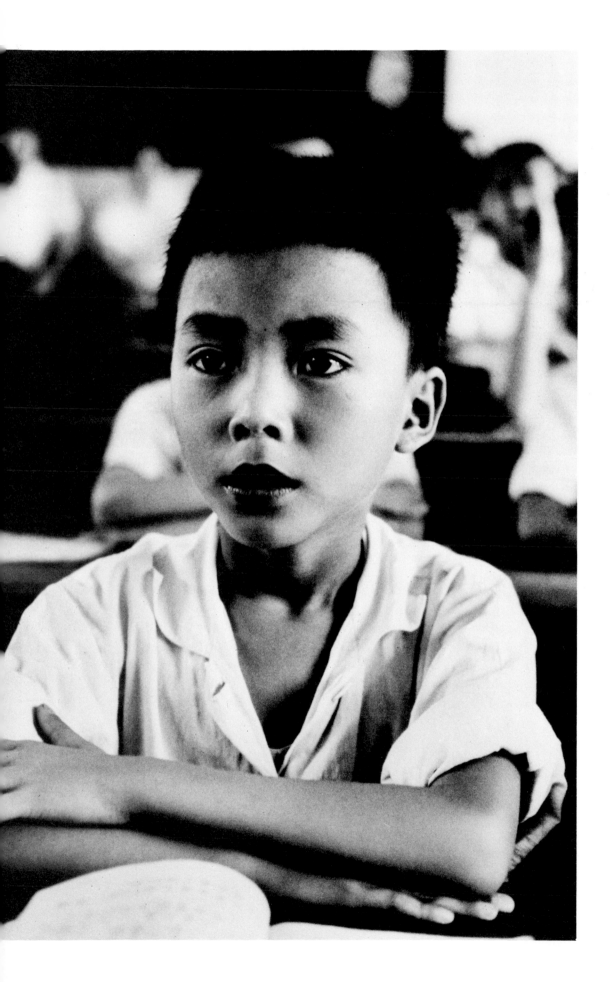

Fu Tan, technical
university in Shanghai

a student sailor
(in blue) studies

my name is
Wang Ming, the

Bright Emperor. I
made the kingdom

shine with dikes
and poplars.

once there were
floods. I planted

saplings, and ghosts
went away

from the village.
after school I

and my friends
in the meadows

are very serious
with young trees

please observe me. see
easily I am wind
of many dynasties,
the history of cypresses
in my walk. now
like rice fields
and water
I am in the center.
look at me so you
and I will not forget

Designed by Tom Coleman